Warcries

Part I: In Combat Theatre

Oh, Beauteous Battlefields of Quiet Sand

July 2003:

Nothing worse than

daylight, under the constant shadow

of wilted-winged mosquitoes. Salted sweat sticking

to our backs.

Fevers made heavier with hushed

Sorrows, embroidering the plentitude

in one thick husk.

The feel of fear unspoken, too commonplace.

The silence, a playground where my terrors

rumbled, wrapping my hairs in a linen muzzle, finely stitched

with a desert crease.

The conflict is Purgatory,

all around us.

Midnight with the Tear-shaped Pillars

Old Arabia breaths blazes. Its Vulcan ashes attach

to my neck. Mules pull apart our bodies. Heralds

recount all tall tales; grotesque!

Invisible tears caress my cheeks.

Into the cold dead womb, I run.

Into Iraq's black ocean, I run.

Soothing is the eager lone night.

The stars blanket this warring desert.

I retreat to them in humble prayer.

If this is a church, then let me be lifted.

<u>It became its own God</u>

I

Fists punch,

hard, cracked, blurred faces.

Bloody knuckles make for

clumsy clubs. Loathing.

II

They no longer serve their

master's doctrines. They only kill to live.

Hands, anointed by

the grace of sandstorms. The caress

of midnight frozen. High flying, defiant.

III

Survivors returning, at the mercy

of their own choking throats. Only

the training keeps the blood from gushing

into the promised land.

IV

Legs worthlessly carry me forward.

I am blessed with a curse.

Pall bearing myself onward.

The end was no resolution.

Migraine

The morning light splinters
into my eye.

I am awake.

Three windows behold
the dawning city, where nothing
is happening abruptly.

God, you were once my only friend.
Now you refuse to call on me.

The whirlwinds blow colder
on the second floor, as if to mock spring.

Little Torments

My body at times, betrays me.
A canteen filled with the chills.

Memories of a berserk,
fawn graveyard filled with sand-spiders,
permeating the world.

Scarlet floods, painting the backdrop black.
The mad battlefields thirsty, bathing,
soaking.

Men die while standing,
Lungs functioning, yet horrors
overwhelm the brain; stand-down!

Flashcards of their skeletons
everlasting in portraits of ink.

My sanity etched across
abandoned brick, quivering rubble.

The Enemy of my Enemy is Myself

A bullet whistles.
One more drop in the pit.
One less soul to claim.
All hallelujahs, haphazardly gone.

Jesus Get Your Gun

It is a heavy burden
to always wear the Kevlar crown.

To be the voice of authority.

It is a sadness never spoken.

It just broods in the eyes.

His intangible force dissolves,
In the brisk rays of the midnight sun.

His dreams crushed in the palm,
of his very own hand.

Being the law jades a man.

Minefield

I wish I could return.
Backwards in time.

Never would I have learned
speech.

Never.

Not one word.

Purity lost.

All began with hate crimes
well thought.

Regurgitated, then superbly spoken.

Boots

My feet ache from
the long, long march.

The vengeful desert sun
hangs high in the virgin sky.

Today I discovered I died
nine years ago.

Reborn into Atlas, I bear
heavy rusted chains.

Dead weights that fester in their
own stew!

Their aromatic horrors
lingering indefinitely.

I inside

This world speaks in judgments;
Spilling ideas into our mouths.
I am emptied. Heartless.

Candles lit.
Raindrops sopped.
Oil pumped.

Monotony repeats.

Each day a pearl strung
Forms the necklace I wear.
Dogtags honorably earned.

Tightly—it chokes.

Shadows of September

I left you alone daughter.

Back when I draped

green fatigues and

blackened boots.

 Wore a rifle for

purpose and protection—

the "horse and pony shows."

I wish I could say it was all

honest work,

defending red, white, and blue.

But that was a grave mistake.

When the killing started,

when the gloves came off,

I was just a little girl again

who wanted more than anything

to come home.

II

It has been a few years

hours, minutes, seconds.

13

I still haven't found the answers.

Only empty questions.

Your angelic face,

scarred no soul.

Your infant hands,

held no malice.

Your pristine feet,

treaded upon no

Nation.

Out there I wished,

I resembled you

child.

Graciousness,

spewed from your lips

as dribbles as you slept.

Small reminders that there

was a God.

Innocence.

Incoming (Coming Home)

I

Hands: worn.

Arms: scarred.

Bodies: saturated.

Blood, sweat.

Those desperate for heroics, suppose

there's never enough to sacrifice.

II

Ravishing rivers, all ravaged.

Bestial bridges, all burnt.

Gave up our spark,

prostituted ourselves.

Been imprisoned ever since.

Responses: The Pity of War and Such Things

I glimpse the gentle pains
of the once recruited lambs.

Their cries, converted into
Hollow-mouthed whimpers.

Begging never to be forgotten
by the passing novel soldiers;
who are loyal only to the failing
revolution.

In the end they failed us all

Preservatives:

These old war wounds
the body carries.

They cradle me.
Spirited hands bathed
in golden spotlights.

All lost treasures,
I hold delicate.

Repercussions:

This great nation extracted us.
Flung us far from peace,
out of infancy.

Into Iraq where we raped
pillaged, plundered.
Survived on chaos, fed on frenzy.

Just to return to a silent hell.
Civilian life not what it seemed.

Too many disappointments
to swallow down.
Rotting inward, barbarously.

We wandering, bewildered souls
search the infinite horizon.

For answers like rain,

Our mouths dry.
Lips chapped.

Heads heavy.
Minds unfurled.

No empathetic ears to listen.
No sympathetic shoulders to cry upon.

Its vision distant, continuous.
As long as the torment.
Forever long.

--In memoriam to the 349 veteran suicides from 2012-2013

Ancestry

I pray we never truly know the sadness of our fathers…

Arrangement

Like it or not, we are all married to death.

Endless Desert, Endless Sand

I

Echoes in my head scream embers
into the opening of my heart.

Love! My ears are burning
from your sonorous winds.

You are a wisping heatwave, relentless.

II

Long ago the rains dispersed.

They have yet to return.

My eyes swollen with broken droplets.

Await release from your invisible,

unforeseen chokehold.

Accidentally Prone

When I walk the emptied streets,
I feel winter's chill. In it I hear the
echo of snapping twigs.

The sound bounces off marble walls,
as if propelled.
Everywhere.

In my knees I feel it most,
even on the days most sundrenched.

It's a white noise.

A muffled clamor.

A frosted touch.

An unjust murmur.

I walk on soft paws,
a frightened cat on sheets of ice.

Slowly its underbelly is chipping.
Cracking.

Unstable.

Part II: At Home, Out of Theatre

Expiation (Why Sunflowers don't Grow in New York City)

The old man,

 a gardener,

your keeper

exclaimed "I can do nothing!"

As the vagrant city

snatches off your petals, loving you not.

In you dear flower, I see myself

once a tall beautiful thing,

now a withering wreck, in need.

But the people pass, moving on.

Your sacrifice unnoticed, unremembered.

No memorials in the gardens.

Only the empty stillness

of your life—uprooted.

A Poem for Reinaldo

No one fights when beauty dies.

Whether it was crushed by human hands
or just with words and undying wills.

There was and always will be
silence.

-Dedicated to Reinaldo Arenas

Foreshadow

I heard the choir
of our breaths.

Moans.
Under nightfall.
Exulted hymns.

Your lungs—inhaling.
Exhaling.

Your touch.

Gentle…
Demanding.

I erupt.

Lucid Remembrance

The hour is twilight.
Gray matter shrieks!

Electric cadences echo.
Long dead, long dead.

The past tiptoes, between dropped rain.
Floored boards wooden bend.
Stony mitts tread softly.

Once I acquiesced in God's desert.
The stillness seldom let me be.
Winds blew wanten desires.

You burrowed them in the tusks of your breasts.
An undiscovered country, in my sunkissed hands.

Your lips to my lips.
The mass of your soul—caught!
Naked.

Your legs spread.
A peach begging to be sucked.

Slurped.
Slit.

The sweet stink of your wet, lying
against me.

Beneath me.
Atop me.

Inside.
Coupled.

Aftermath

I

I bit down on the ties of my tongue.
Knowing what most would think.

Don't ask—I accepted the lie.
Devoured it.
Swallowed every spoonful.

Don't tell, don't tell, don't tell!
Best not question.
Best not question.

Honor.
Truth.
Law.

The enemy shares my fish tank.

II

Too many sombered faces.
Mostly sleepwalkers—Lancaster...
There one day too many.

Not a good day when I saw her face.
Five days past the event.
Detailed for clean up, incidentally.

She witnessed the black ash.
Tasted scarlet iron.
Smelled how death plumes—unilaterally.

Debris flew high, low, surrounding.
Grits made a home, in her browning teeth.
Sandpits engulfed sunlit beams.

Smile no longer ivory.

Glass stripped her fingertips.
Bled into the cuticles.
Shards nestled forming unwanted friendships.
Presence irremovable.

She groceried the scatterboned appendages.
A blood-soaked jigsaw at hand.
She became a doppelganger of herself.
The original, I never saw again.

My Narrow Escape

Martyr's Monuments.
The mortar rounds.
Kaboom, Kaboom, Kaboom!

For 3½ hours.
Explosion after explosion.
After explosion.

Trampling in each others
footsteps.

A caravan of clumsy elephants.

Followed by the promises of a clown.

My Captain assured us the convoy
would be safe.
His delusions of authority ran deep.

He assumed we all were playing by the same rules.
Death cheats.
War has no referee.

Initiation

Spawn of the dust.
Populate 'longside the roads.

They sell liquid gold by the gallon full.

Their dreams forsaken.
Galvanized.

A hardboiled egg overdone.
Cooked to fatigue.

Bellies swelled with malnourishment.
Hearts and minds—unwon.
Emptied.

We crucified them children that year.
That year—and every year since.

Of these crimes none speak.
None dare shake the cage.

Victors are the writers of history.

Mongrels

We were apes gone mad.
Routines carved in, gouged out the soul.
Shells took their place.

Anticipation steroided us.

Started dragging our knuckles.
Men no longer men.
Women no longer women.

I had heard the rumors.
Alpha Co. 1st Sergeant had an itch—to kill.

Couldn't get at the Iraqis soon enough.
Bringin' the thunder in, heavy. Heavy.
Wasn't 1st AD's job anymore though.

"Mission accomplished."
Invitation to the dance, retrieved.
Regained. Revoked.
Rescinded. Rescinded.

Restructured from combat.
Now engagement peace party.

Oh how, his palms must have sweated.
How his triggerfinger must have seethed.
On those long nights without fire.
His rifle next to him, limp; cold.

Didn't sit well.
To be an "Angel of Mercy."
I suppose he bore resent.

Like the fox I had seen once.
Resembled anything but.
Had a xylophone for ribs.

Swift through our lampposts, on all desperate fours.
That night hunger made music.

Same went for the downy dogs.
The roughed howls of those he shot.
1st Sergeant—Alpha Co.
Following orders—with "uncomposed," childlike glee.

I close-breasted those rumors.
Because of his eyes.
Coveted malevolence, brighten in its joy.

They were a chilly northern skyscape.

In them, a lasting sight you'd see of death.
Carnivorous starvation.
The gargling of houndless voices.
And his drooly grin.

Baited Breath

The rocks.
Good for a makeshift bed.

I was pancaked in sandpowder.
Desert sugar—my blanket.

Kevlar capped tight 'round the head.
My pillow. No feathers to spare.

This dull sleep.
One of the last.
I dare not dream, to live.

In three days time.
One step closer.

Home again.
Home again.
Home again.

Pandas in a Bamboo Cage

I am a tempest.
Full of questions—no relent.

Gagged.
Black bagged.

Dumbstruck.

These few years in between years.
Enlighten nothing.

Sharpened Pens & Poisoned Inks

I am writing this,
eyes closed.

Mind full.

Pen opened, by the beat of
the living light.

These words are a noose
from which I gladly hang.

The end comes gently to those
with fool's courage.

Greet it with a smile!

Sobered

I awoke upwards to a clear, gray sky
looking to be without the touch of a molten sun.

My fingers no longer possess their prints,
my feet no longer impose their tracks.

The blue skyward dome howled so wildly,
it shook! Listen!

No one hears its desperate cries—but me.

Beyond a Doubt

The brightness lies.

Within my soul,
love is tarnished.

Eventually I destroy
the anchor that binds us
together.

I cannot help that I am a warrior!
I cannot help that I am a warrior!
I cannot help that I am a warrior!

Living is the Hardest Thing

"Where was your child when you deployed?"
"How long did you stay away?"
"Did you ever think you wouldn't survive?"
"Did you ever kill anyone?"

These questions hunt me down like a boar
in broad daylight.

My apartment is silent,
but I can still feel the pounding
of the mortars.

The boom of the bombs.

These sounds rattle
my cage, pushing against
my sanity.

Each day threatens to
crumble the walls.

Sandstorms whip nightmares
around my throat. Breathe!

I cannot.
The air is brittle.

Trails of sweat dance
with traces of my tears
of salt. All left to conjure

a reality that is a dream
before dying.

Transfusions

These days, I stare too long at the sun.

Mirrored pools spiral.
They tell me,
I've lost all the color in my eyes.

You; me,
I can no longer gage the differing.

The ground is an overused baking sheet.

Allowing the brain to be conquered.
By blood.

Contemplations Beyond

Maybe there is a God.
Not above me.
Cradled in a floating blob of sky.

Not beneath me.
Sweltered in a coffin patch of ground.

But within me.
Within me.
Within me.

Rough Boys, Tough Boys

Crowds crowd street in a steamy, perspired haze.
Alarmingly loud, for a burnt out avenue.
Forced on this scavenge.

No choice. Goodwin's turn.

Fellows in Bravo Co. thirsty.
Desperate for neighborhood treats.
Hands irritably shooken with money.
Pitstop at Baghdad grocery.

Stood guard on side of road.
A line of us, a wall.
Massed men shouting back, forth.
Introverted struggle; keep hands steady.

Aggression surrounds, like porcupine needles.
Festering sun.
Beams transport me backward.
Almost like Brooklyn homed summers, past.

Spurts of fire hydrants.
Pressured water smacking skinny, naked legs.
Flailing hands.

Squeals.
Hollers.
Tin can filters.
Ice temps raining down on passing cars.

Never feared the summer before.
Crowds neither.
But now…

Gatherings here, alien somehow...

No cars.
No squeals.
No laughs.
No women; no children.
Just testerone.

Intensed.
Engrossed.
Dangerous.

Feral cats ready to pounce.
Claw.
Gut.

And me.
Me.
Me; right in the thick.

Outnumbered.
Outnumbered.
Outnumbered.

Allies.
Enemies.
Both ready to play the Spaded Ace.

Lightweight, Heavyhitter

Guard duty again.
Pulled.

As if my name was the only one,
written in the hat.

He seemed nice for a wild card.

Number 86 on Bush II's list.

Dare not think on who he was.
What he did to earn his place.
What would happen once he got,
to where he was going.

No need to think.
Can't hesitate.

If he gives a problem.
Would have to shoot.
Never took a life before.

Knew how to avoid catasphes
In New York.

Not New York though.
Another ghetto battlefield.

Hands feel bloodied already.

Boys of Summer

His voice—a caramel filling.
Clogging the stoned ventricles.
Sweeting the sadness.

Minion.
Traitor.
Sandnigger.

Endured hatred from his people.
Tolerated distain from the coalition.

Could not be helped.
Need to feed wife. Kids.

Hanging by a strained thread.

Earned distinguishment as a Chemist.
Spoke several languages, including French.

Uppity education.
What good would it do you now, sir?

His life flashed.
Escaped into the sunset.
We exchanged silences.
He sighed disappointment. I breathed it in.

I knew his story before he spoke it.

Sinking…
Something about to burst…

Unbelievable!
Termitic teeth munching!
My brain must be made of wood!

Cannot let the infestation spread.

Demoted my sympathies.
Dulled my senses.
Search frantic; distraction!

Floodnumbed the mind.
Glutton for nonsense.

His voice trailed away.
Lonesome.
Weakness amputated.

Radio

They are soot caked manikins.
Bobble dolls.
Heads moving—out of control.

If you pretend hard enough,
it's like watching a bad action flick.

Fear keeps me sturdy though.
In the now of the now.

In the near distance, I study them.
Lips chapped, peeling—in fervor
of a good lickin'.

Hands tied, rickety in my throat.
Can do nothing but my duty.

He is pinned, I say.
Over the radio.

Break.
Response: Report situation.

I spy. I do. I report.
I get the distance wrong.

But I see high, almost from above.
Binoculars startling clear.
Peering into this darkness.

The black pistol in his hands.
Pointing ahead…the shadows.

The beauty of his garment flowing—a summer Thobe.
Pristine cloth, draping the night.

His tracks, soft marks.

A gazelle's step.

Then…

Gunfire, gunshots.
Pow, pow, pow!!!!

Whizzing.
Back.
Forth.

Break.
Report: Not our problem.

Oh…

Revelation

Justice is nothing but a word.
A busted machine slothfully working itself.
Into an early grave.

Thwarted

Laryngitis, whittling my resolve.
Decades of story, obscured 'neath scar tissue.
Stunting a voice in its prime.

Brethren

I

I will drink of your suffering.

Partaking of your cries

as if they were blessed teardrops.

Sipping them as salted teas

flavored with remorse.

Of our stories only the dead will speak.

In quiet arias.

Harmonies lifted.

II

Threads of terror, oh how they do bind.

Righteously woven with violent hands

Strands finer than the finest of silks.

Plentiful scars are ripples.

Like old fingers painting,

the blackened ocean.

A fitting paradise for

the warring heavens.

Tremors

Stumbling through the gaps.
Each tread, a chance.
Cracks expanding—creating universes.

Plummeting.

Declaration of Independence

No matter what anyone says,
I know this in my heart.

I am no heroine.
I am merely a survivor.

Who could not die for something.
She misunderstood.

Land, Sky

I am camouflaged in old scars.
Forged by the white-noise of my smile.

Dismembered wails horde.
A pounding thunderstorm.

The gulf between you and I.

Echoes in November

Veteran's Day.
Countdown 'til celebrations.
I shudder.

Here.
Build a fog.
Best just lose yo'self.

The memories—immemorial,
leaves bile as an aftertaste.

The Army's lingering impression upon me.
Filthy imprints.
Wash, but can't get clean.

North.
South.

East.
West.

War.
Cinematic.
Reoccurring.

Life stabbing into an open wound.
Repeatly.

Remorseless.
'til it passes, nothing real.

Defector

I cannot go backwards.
Cannot be lulled to sleep.
I have seen the darkness of man,
I am awakened.

Unsaid (Confession)

Mouth.
Ziptie.
Black and tightening.

Around lips that refused.
Refused the peace of shutting.

witness.
As the prisoner moaned.
The "Meal Ready to Eat" bag went,
over his head.

Covering his face.

The temp that day,
had to be at least 110.

No more like 120.

The searing stalked our backs,
even in doors.

Imprisoned within a prison.
"This must be hell."
Internal monologues mumbled.

Silence. Then the buildup.
Swaying, back and forth.
Slow, perpetuating.

Faster, faster.
Then…
Wallowing…

Inhuman.
Indiscernible.
Wallowing, wallowing.

Agitating the other cellmates.
Shouts in Arabic.

I assumed they retorted,
"Yo' shut the fuck up!"

'cause that's how we all felt.

I wouldn't be moved,
to fury, however.

I would just sit.
I would just sit, read.

I would just sit, gawk.
I would just sit, watch a movie.

By then, I knew how to live in a hole
where his hollering couldn't reach.

The other soldiers—female guarded duty.
Boy, how those white girls would powertrip.

Now they had a hold on me.
Gave me the quakes.
Somethin' awful.
Was like waiting for a grenade to blow.

Banshees.
Screeching at the inmates.

Batons banging.
Ratting the chainlinked fence.

Hearing those noises,
compulsed inward cringes.

Sounds sometimes paranoid me,

his very day.

 and the other black girls.
Never did that.
Never lost cool.
Not on my watch.
Not once.

Maybe 'cause we knew.
We saw.
How they looked.

They resembled us.
Family distanced by time.
This war separated us by nation.
But shade united us.
Akin.

Therefore, I wasn't perturbed.
Disturbed.
Disrupted.
Or afraid.

Not even by the prisoners habits.
How they wiped their assholes,
with their hand—no toilet paper.

I believe it was the left.
They ate only with the right.
Everyone else—unanimous disgust.
I was glad they tried to cleaned with water.

But that one.
That one dude.
That prisoner.

Something about him.
Seared through the gray.

Admiring, his freedom.
His uninhibited candidness.

This comes in abundance to those,
who are either blessed or cursed.

Either way he leaned, the road
led in one direction.

Berserk.

Fact.
He was hated because of this.

Truth.
He was hated for so much more.

He was hated because he was there.
Hated for being an Iraqi.

Hated for hates sake.
Hated because he could not be controlled.
Hated because he could not be dominated.

Hated because he reflected,
what we had done.
To that nation.

Hated because his spirit would not die,
even though his mind certainly did.

And when the Sergeant First Class' hands
reached over and put the ziptie on to
Muzzle the howler I was pinched by the irony.

Of one black man enslaving another.
Of this sin I have barely spoken.

Confession—I became accompliced to
his action.

This deed inhumane.

 despised this moment of cowardice.
Speak up I did not.

Instead caring about my own hide.
I did nothing.

Knowing that.
The man—insane, irritating.
Dangerous—maybe.

Was still a man nonetheless.
And could have died.

From heat.
Or shock.
Asphyxiation.

Replays.
Over.
My head…

The tape records.
Rewinds.
Focus.
I am volcanic with fear.

Didn't rock the boat.
Stayed in my hole.

I lied.
Nothing more to say.

The others.
Their unison.

They were bigger than me.

Responses

Please don't speak to me of the greater good.

Goodness is my half-recollected dream.
It's silvery hooks fish through charred
memories.

I depart them into swollened palms.
Once mighty; strong.

Surviving decay in one instant.
Falling to it the next.

Clouded eyes beseeching understanding.
In their own juices confused brains swim.

Slaughterhouse rules.
10 years collected upon the pelts.

Fading the wool—emasculating the lambs.

They beg—remorse over me fondly;

Yet the children here are spoiled.

Either unlearned or gloried by wars, warriors, hero-worship.

All fingers point.
Hands invigored risen over airfluffied chests.

Gestures.

Laughter.

Salutes.

The soldiers pass.

Their lives shackled to legends.

Fallacy

I tilt my head to the side.
Squint my eyes.

Slightly grin.

I practice this—until it becomes
reflexive.

But today, for some reason
I am tired.

Of lying.

My sadness is not a pond.
Or a lake.
Nor a river.

It is an underground ocean.
At times a geyser, it springs.

So much heat.

No matter what it is there.
In 'neath me.

Always.

Knowing this brings intense sorrow.
Stating this gives me, hope.

It is hefty.
Weighs on the heart.
Survival.

Surviving.

Love me as is.

In time, I promise
we'll carry.

We'll carry.

Strange Things Happen'd

Barbarous.
Slobbering grunts.
Language lost.

Chivary dead.

Gallant pretenses.
Exchanged pleasentries.

Holding on to civilized principles.
Our actions heroic—regarded no meaning.

I remember…before that happening.

Men, in my unit acclimated their own way.
Some hid from the heat.
Others sheltered into idled work.

A handful most times, would not bathe.

They sat with the stench.
Encrusted, 'casing the skin.
Dust, sweat, blood, piss…

Shit.

All—a proud coat of arms.
Each sculpted to perfection.
Grime of the desert.

Made it shine; polished.

Me, myself
wanted no such aromas.

Bathing twice a day,
changing uniforms often.
never felt—clean.

Cracking like an eggshell.
I couldn't keep spying the same
faces.

Their eyelids wide,
famished times—no fucks.

Ciphering more carnage,
than the phosphorous heat.

Sunken skeleton mauraders.
Their eyes were always watching.

Those were the coldest moments.
Trapped in the deserted hemisphere,
still reaching for warmth.

Some bit of light to fire the blood.
Something…comforting.

Stand down!
Observe your surroundings.
Don't let your secrets, leak.

When you hear the growls,
the starving dogs—best play dead.
Stick to this plan.
They'll soon lose interest.

I will win.

No such luck, all the time though.
Attacks flank, comers out of no where.

I remember…maneuvering.

The shape of his penis—no foreskin.
Exposure—he had no problem with this.

Erected—protruding veins.
Coated brown, as chocolate.

He wanted me to suck it.
He said this "knowing" I would.

Men of high rank, parked their asses
on gold posts.

Those beneath, were to act accordingly.

Instead I made jokes.
Played bewildered.
Doe eyed.
Timid.

He hissed—knotted frustration.
Mistook my cunning—for prudishness.

Was not so lucky with you though.
You who I took as friend.
Should have seen you coming.

Trust.
A great weakness, in outland.

Played the game, like a master.
Plucking my strings.

Cornered me with sorry weights.
Everything flipsided.

Dizzied me.

remembered…very little.
Bits, pieces.
Chopped, screwed.

Puffs of your breath.
Stroking my neck, my ear.

You were the bad wolf,
huffing my name.

Your body pressure.
A hammer pounding.

Pounding.

Flattening.

My body rigamortised.
The ceiling morphied.
A blackhole had formed.
The sight.

Teleported into darkness.
Stuck like molasses.

From it, I never blinked.

Part III: I See the a World

On the Promised Death of Tomas Young

We all became savages out there.

Sucking the marrow from existence.
As if feeding off of oysters.

It was all we could do to salvage
it.

But not you.
You never even got the chance.

Strange.
Your injuries.

Decaying your body.
Preserved something…

Deeper.

More pure.

You were spared one horror.
By bullets.

Yet, stuffed.
Clayed into another.

On that day, I wonder
what you remember.

Every time I think of

Baghdad…

I see rows, columns.
Features people collapsed.
Emaciated.

God was I ice-numb,
way back when.

I try to say it was commonplace.
Something I "had to be."

Now.
Sparks of truth, shoot.
I am thrown.
Ping…
Pong.

You saw through it early.
For our protection—bullshit!

How I envy you—slightly.

Wisdom.
I have learned one assured thing.

Endingly,
it does no justice.

No good.

Enlightenment sheds no rays.
I still cry out.
A nightmared sheep.

Breaking the glass ceiling.
Grants no wishes.

I am as loved,

unloved as I have ever been.

Surely, this is the same for
you.

As for the Iraqi people.
This shared experience,
etched in our blood.

This does not make us innocent.
We are just less guilty—our puppetmasters.

They snooze well.
Clutching their riches—religiously.

The whole world.
Aloof.

It only took ten years.
A guise of chrystaline build.
What monsters.
What monsters.
Using liberty, just to enslave.

Guilt.
Grips our pearled hands.
Tarnishes our toddlered palms.

For oil.

Control.

Wealth.

Superfluous!

You more than most know,
you can't take any of that shit with you.

To Chelsea Manning (A Letter Unsent)

I knew a hero much like you once.
He was in the Army, Bravo Company 501st
In the Forward Support Battalion. He served.

With me.
Except I was in Supply.
He was a Mechanic.
He had a wife, had just become a father.
When he deployed.

He was a Specialist.
His name was Tripp.

Tripp.
He was a good man.
He was a good man,
that Tripp.

I cannot recall his first name.
Till this day.
I still try though. It's funny.
You know how the training stays.

With you.
With me…

But, I digress.
I was talkin' about…
About?

Tripp. Yes.
He was a good man.
A hero.

Like you my friend.
I mean with little differences.

Minor.

Minorities—lines…
 have yet to draw.
 have yet to figure out, which
side I fall upon….

 suppose that's how it goes.
The story of my life.
Can't seem to work out the
kinks…

Between.
In.
Sideways.
Entering.
'Xiting.
Under.
Along.
Laying.

With me…

Forgive me.
I keep losing my place.
My mind.

It wonders sometimes.
I suppose too many months.
Left stagnant.

Those desert memories…
Still reservin' their place.

Again, Tripp.
You alike in heroism.
He savin' seven lives.
Taking a bullet in his shoulder.
The right I believe.

Losing blood, some tendons.
Nerves.
Muscle.
Still…
Drove those seven to safety.

And you?
We all know what you did.
You did what Tripp, would
have done.

You too drove the truck home.
Found a safe space.
Despite your loss.

You kept going.
Because of you, we sleep safely.

But he, like you.
You, like him.

Suffered.
Suffer.
Are sufferin'.

He got a Purple-hearted, shinny
(for his troubles).

Along with an ass load of pills;
perscripted for pain.

You.
I just heard.
God.

God.
Unfair, unfair.
UnFUCKINGfair!!!!

couldn't believe it myself.
Your mother, father, family,
friends.

You.
You.
You...

Jesus!
How you all must have wept.

And I can't wrap, wrap.
Wrap...
My head, it swells around this.

All these lies, for all these years...
So much...
So much...

It almost makes me pray to be
ignorant, again.
God, give me a sign.
Some reprieve.
A ray of hope.
Be.

With me.

At the foot of my bedside.
So I can sleep sound.
Dreamin' up spaces.

Where Tripp holds his
son proud.

And on tall legs you can, will,
Are walkin' stout.

Free.

Iraq

I realize now that almost every O.I.F. vet I know,
cannot even speak your name,
without distain.

It's sticky stink stuck on the pulp,
of their red, ripe—beefy tongues.

I can still hear the caroling of your prayers.
Reminds me of a mater's lullabies.
Each sing, song-silence an echo hovering...

Just above my head.

I no longer dream when I sleep.
Pink pills, and your drowned laughter...
They have taken care of that.

Sons, daughters.
Both beautiful in their slumbering graves.
Children of the dying earth.

Inheritors of the new ghetto.
I have something to tell you.
It shall be harsh, because it is truth.

Your playgrounds are now our landfills.
Our dumpsters, your mattresses.
All too well I know the sight of desolation.

Underneath the dust covered tracks.
Where you and I buried—your one, solitary tear.
When flickering lights where our alter posts.

We shared the same skin.
The same face.
Our shadows young-elderly, and forgotten.

Crossed and have never unlinked.
Under this sky you will die—mistaken.

My, theirs, our visits were false ones.
I collapsed in sadism, erasing.

My origin.
Forgetting.
Once, I was born of it too.

59993280R00047

Made in the USA
Charleston, SC
18 August 2016